Dentist Swears

Swear Word Coloring Book for Ranting & Relaxing

By

S.B. Nozaz

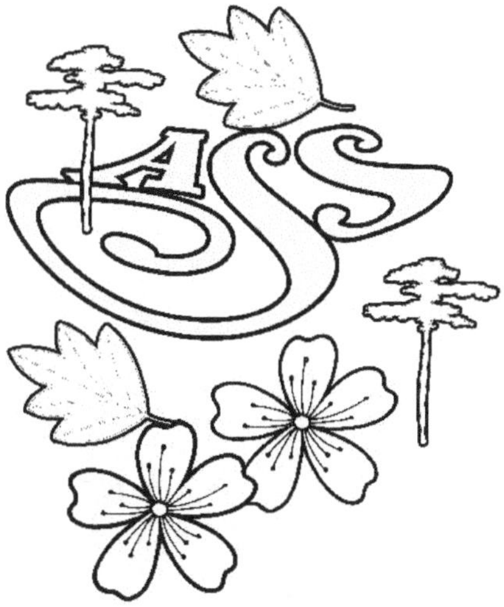

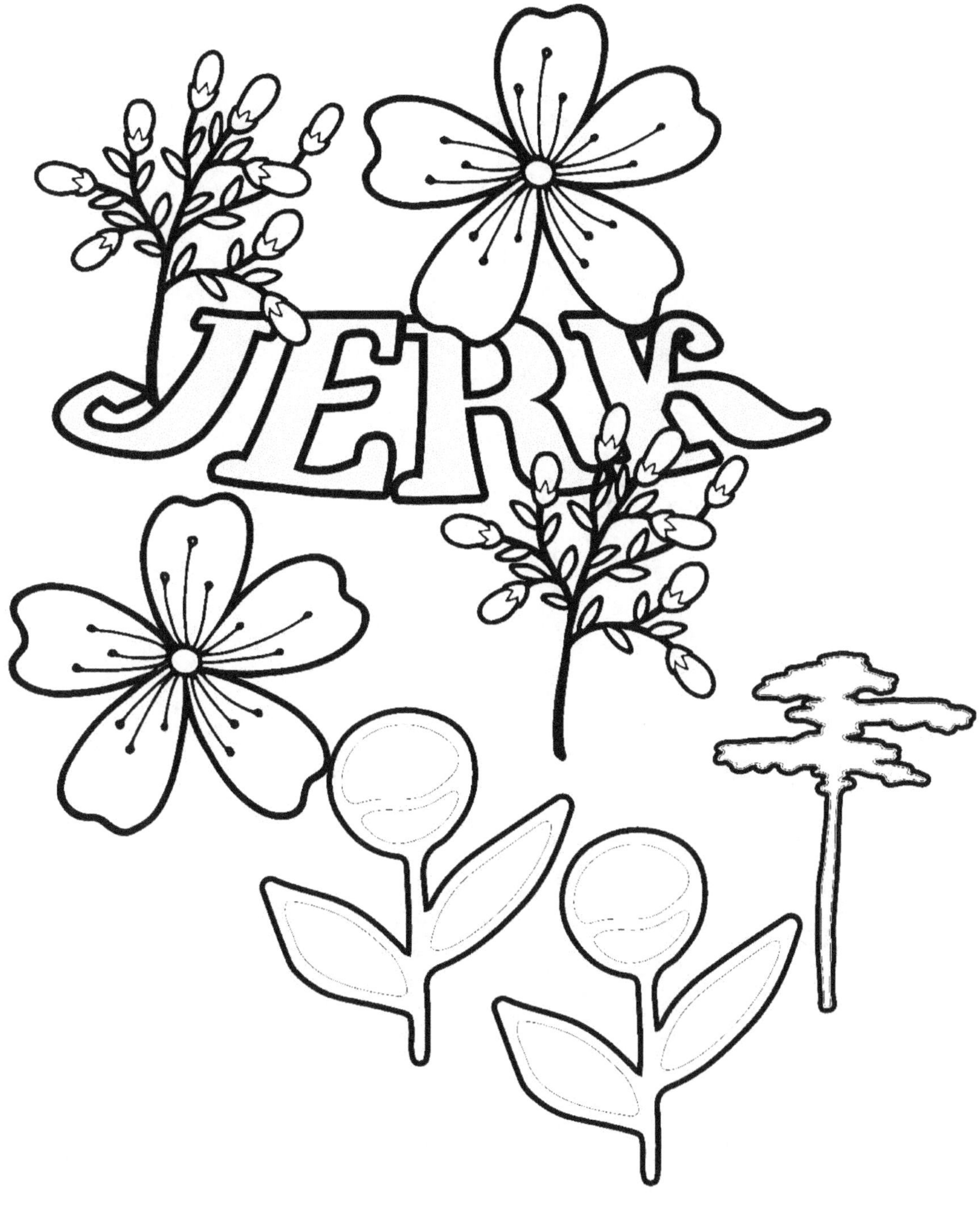
JERY

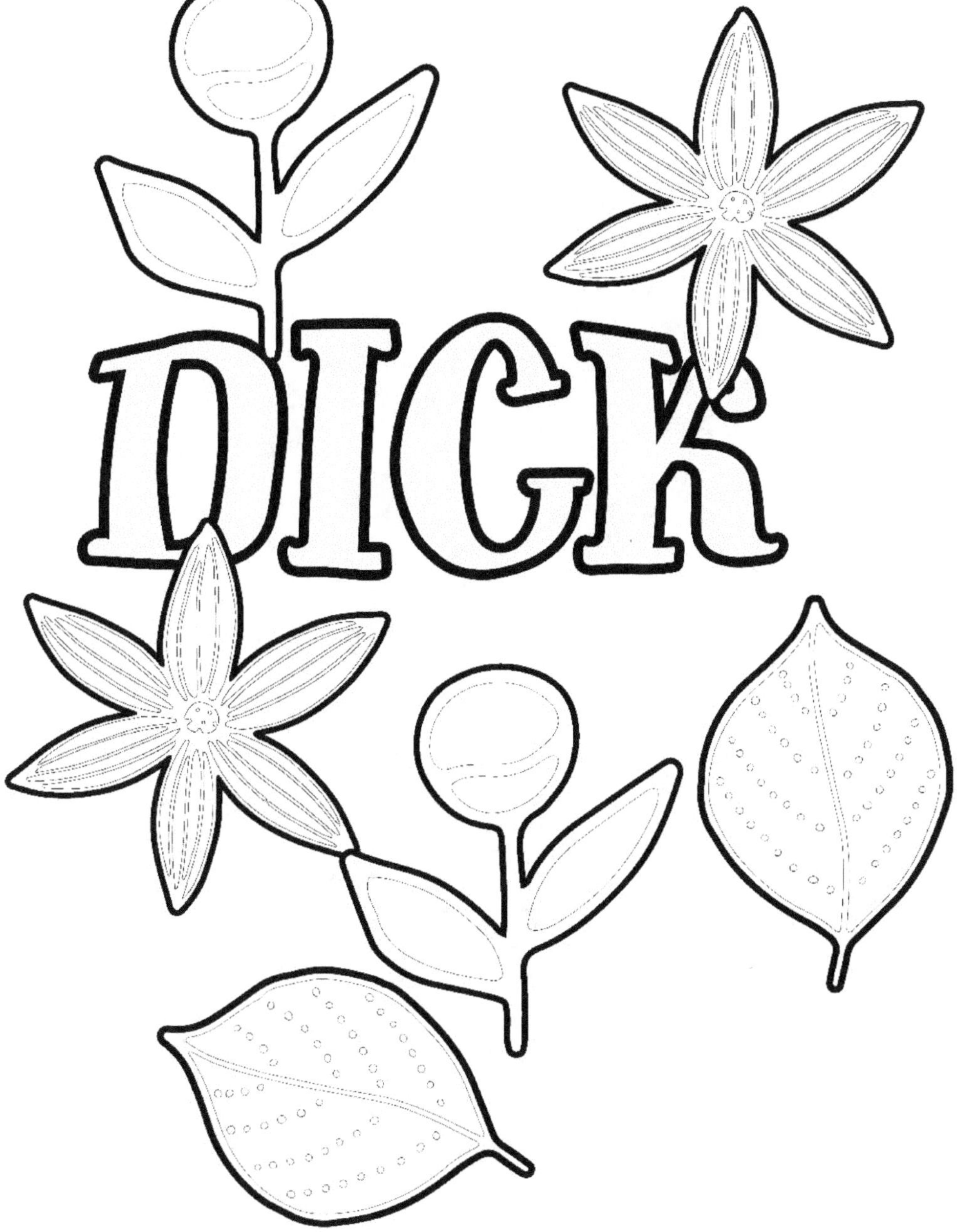
DICK

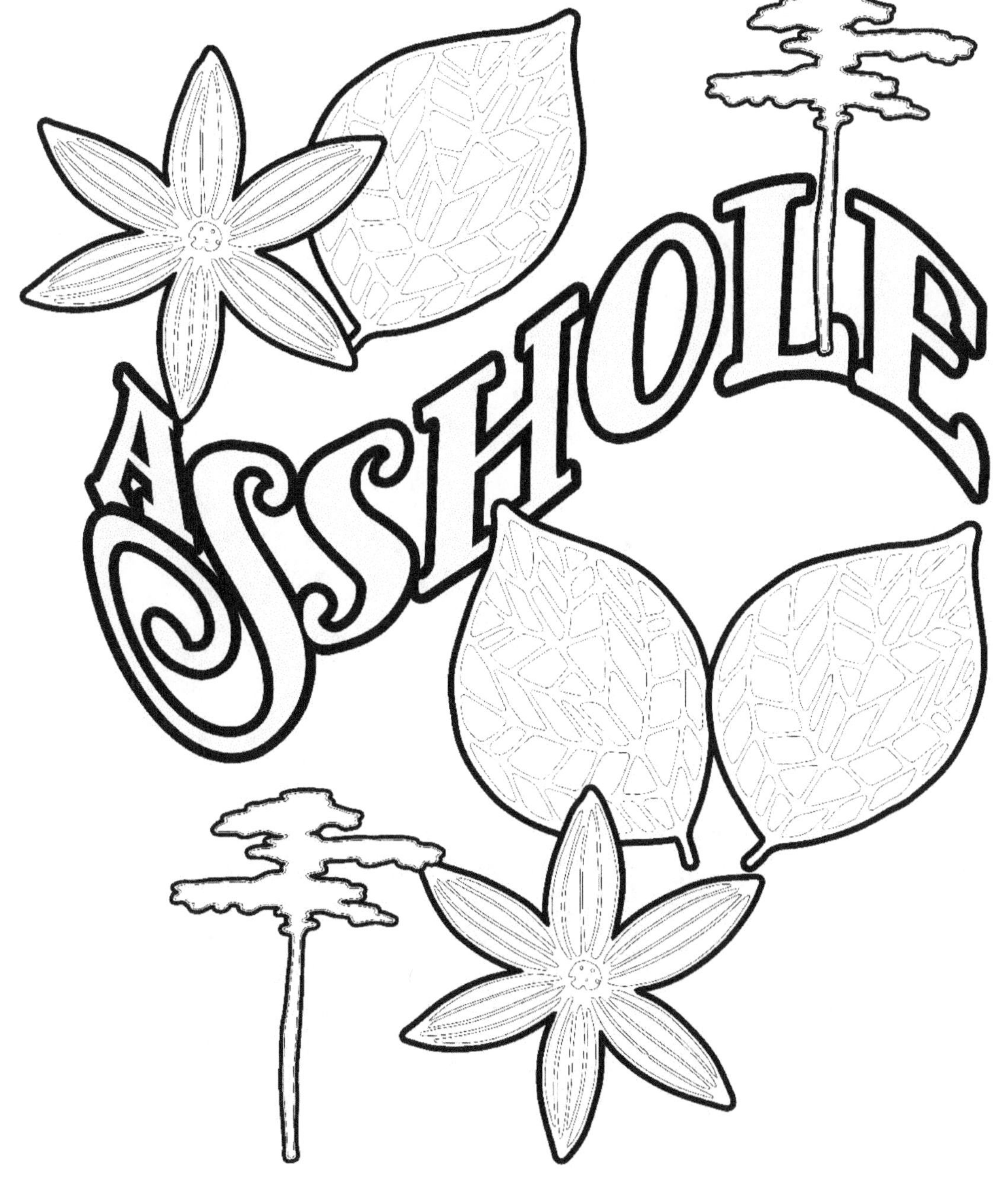
ASSHOLE

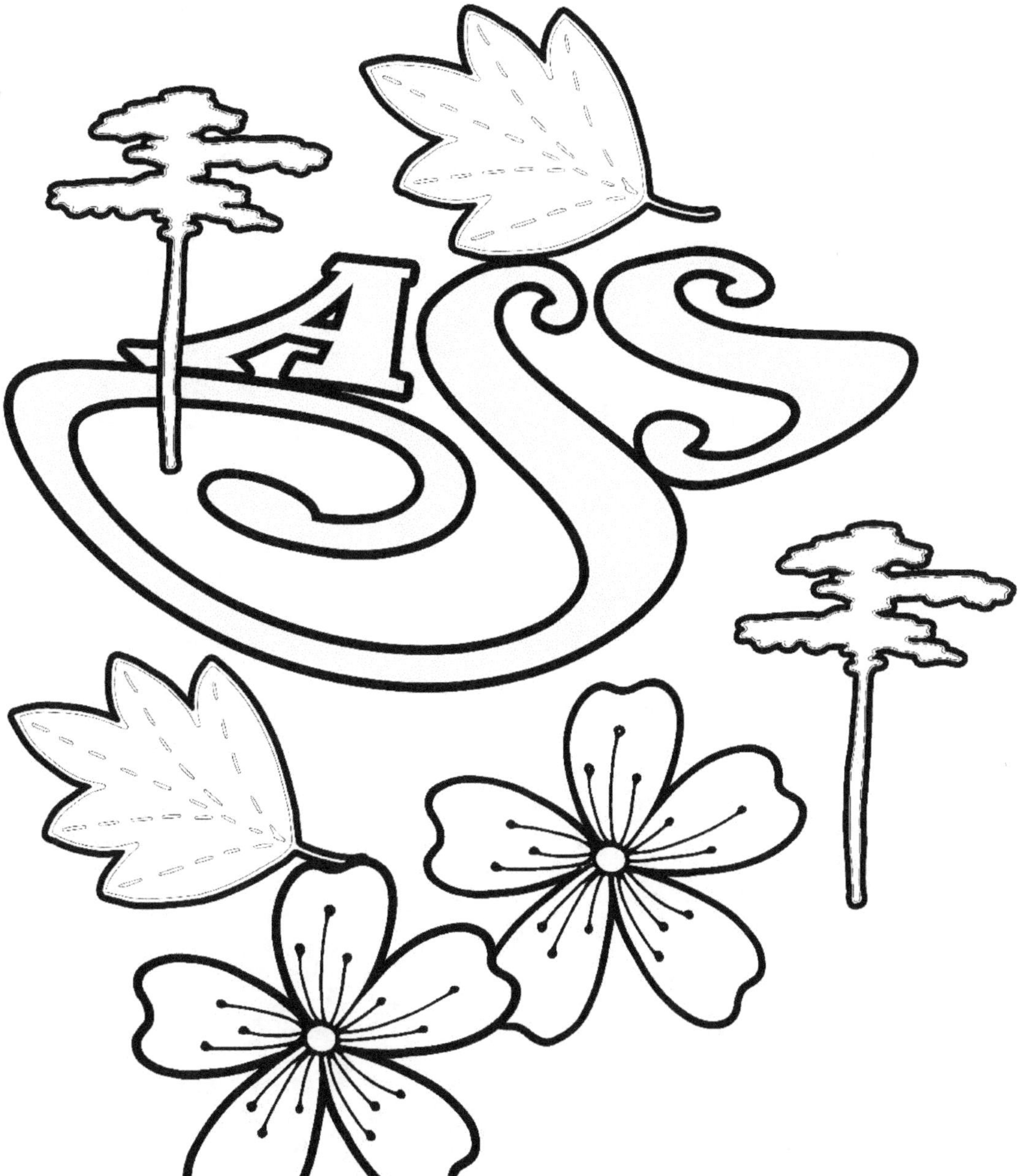
ASS

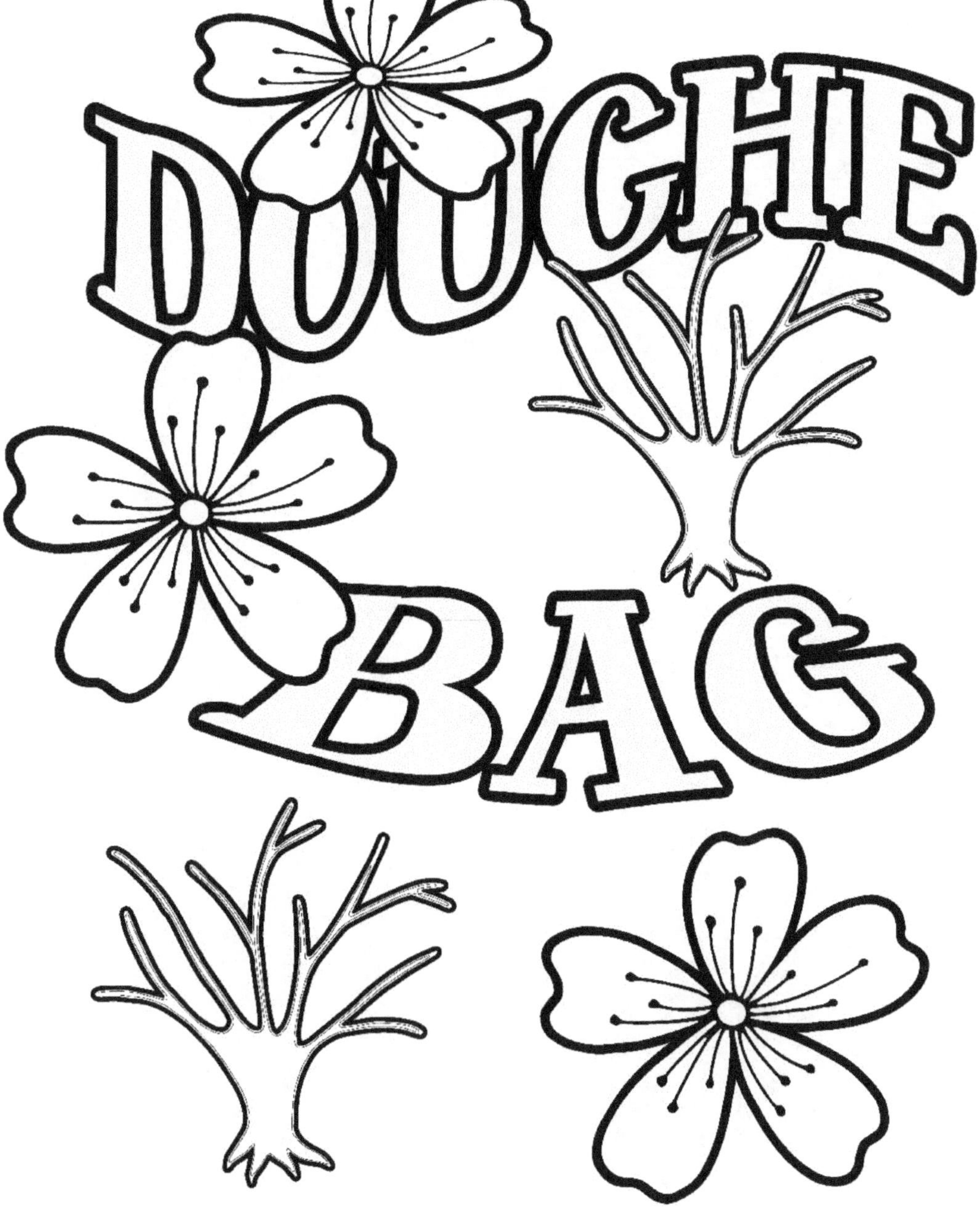
DOUCHE
BAG

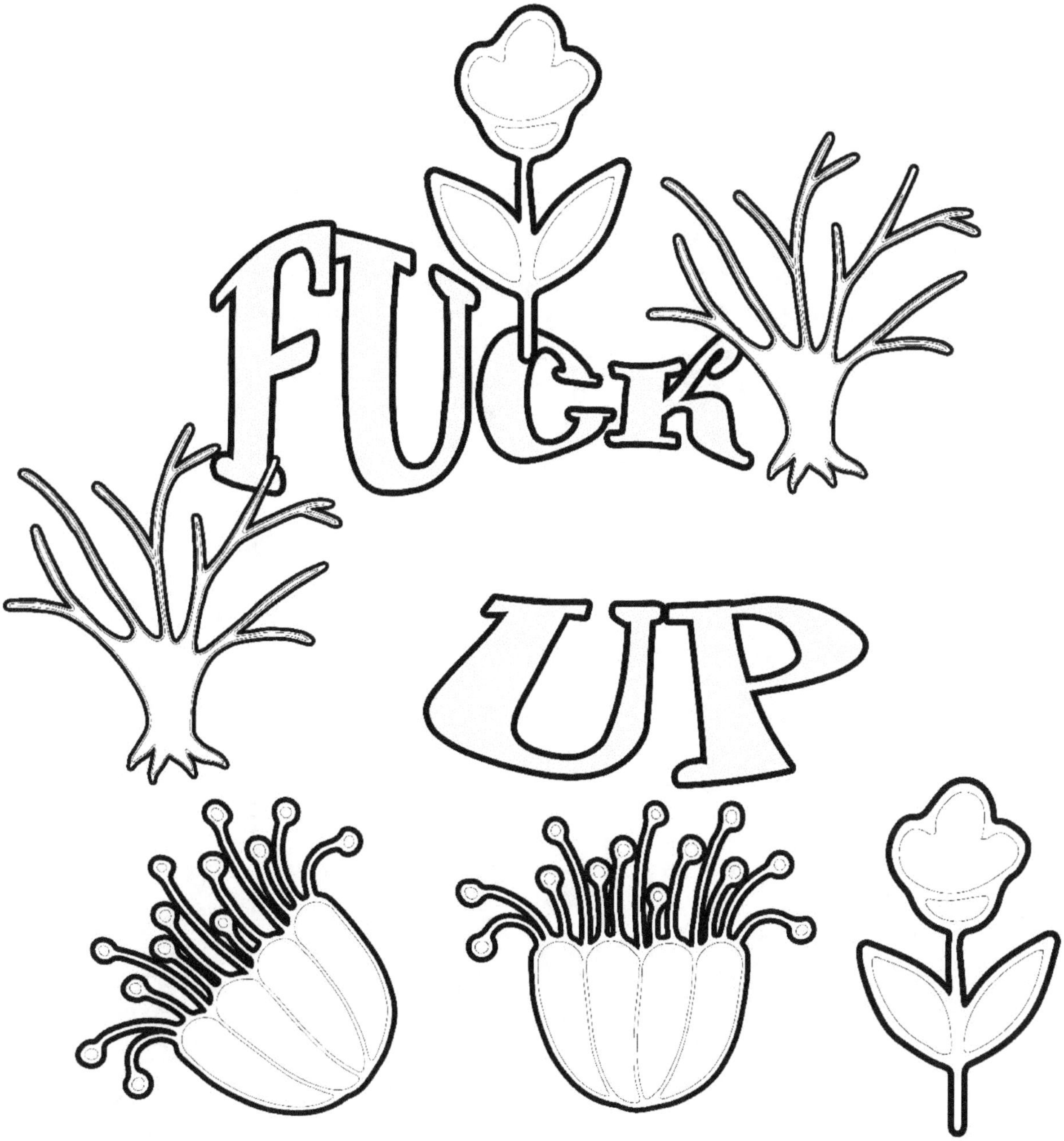
FUCK
UP

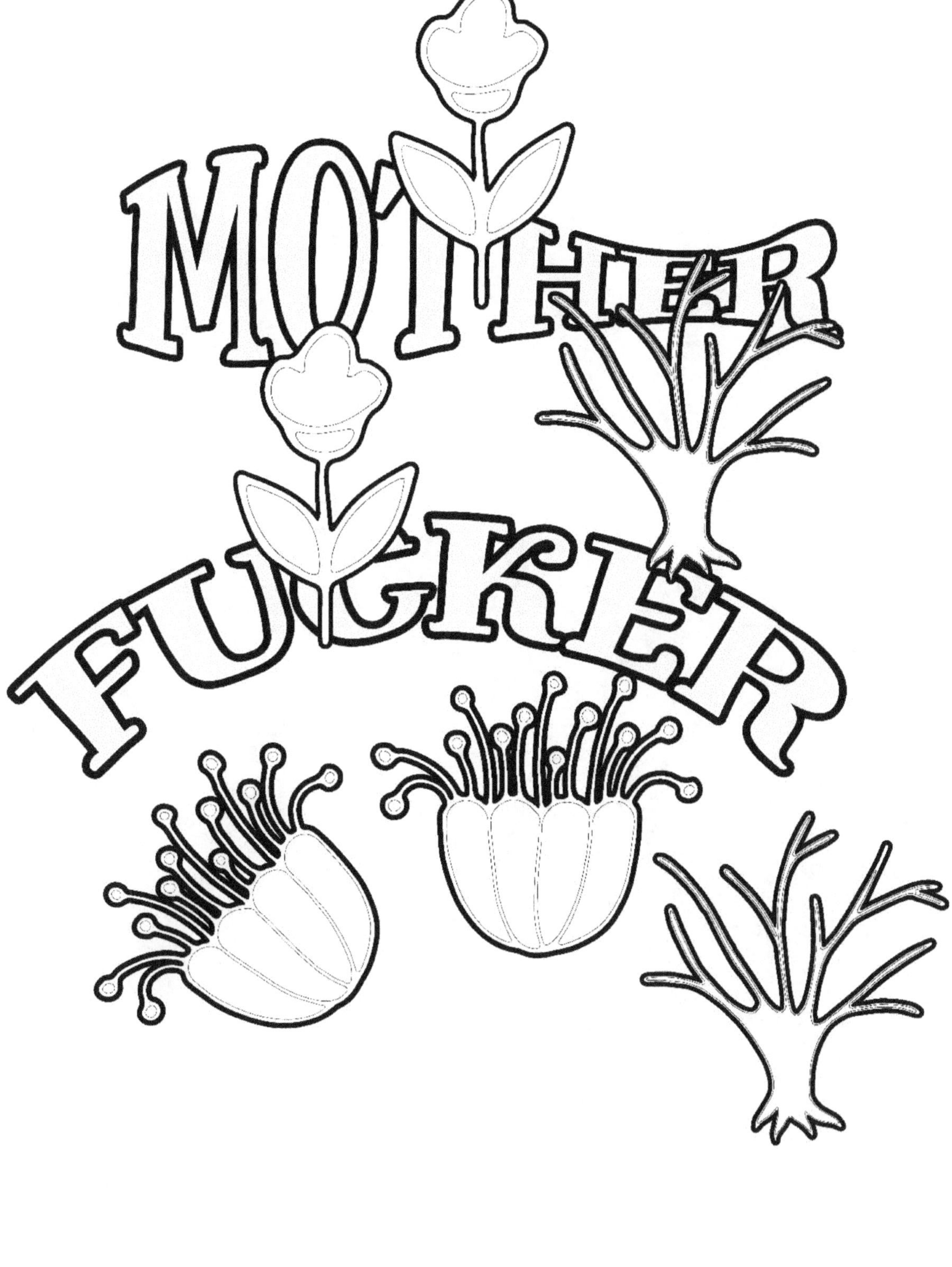
MOTHER
FUCKER

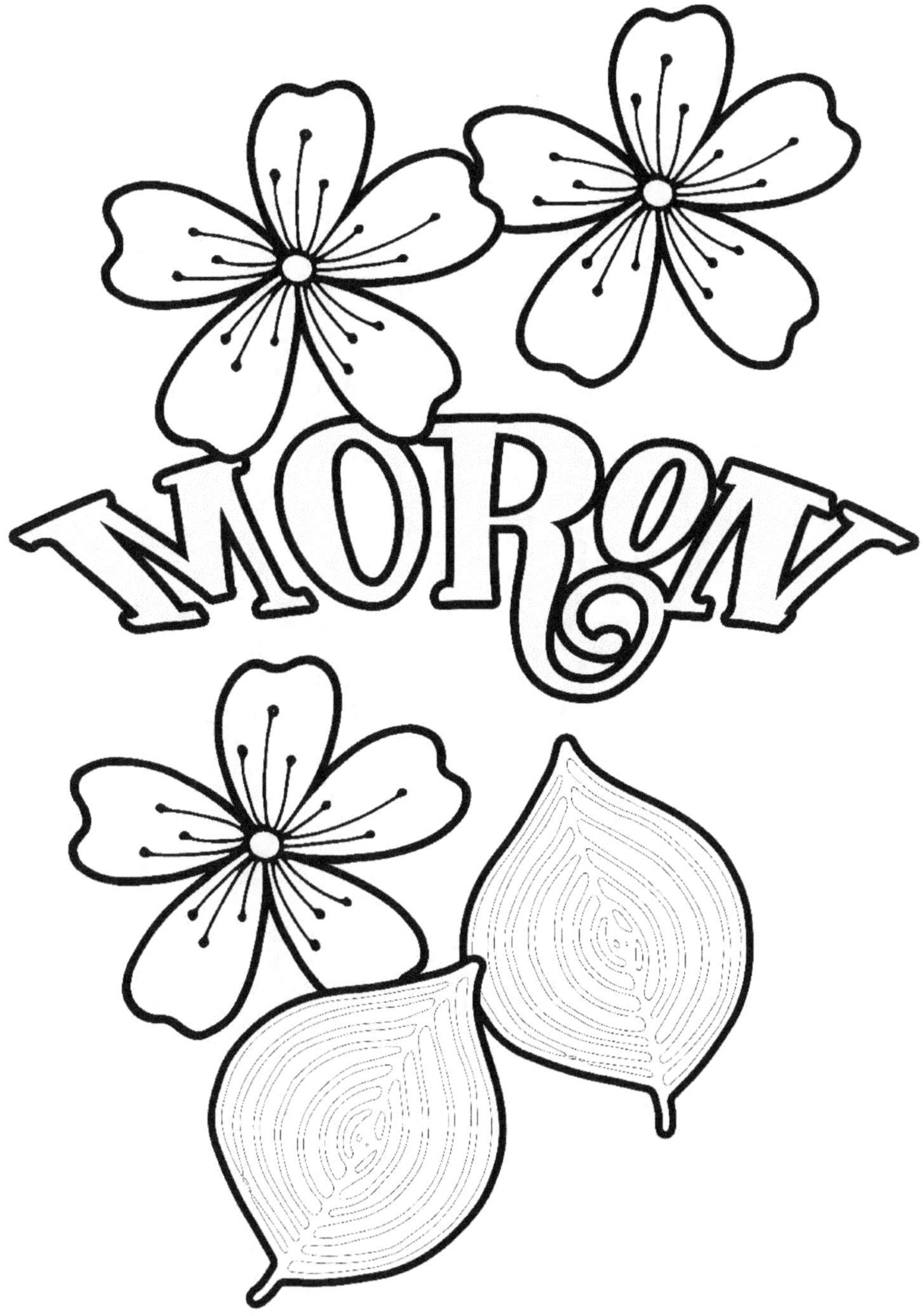
MORON

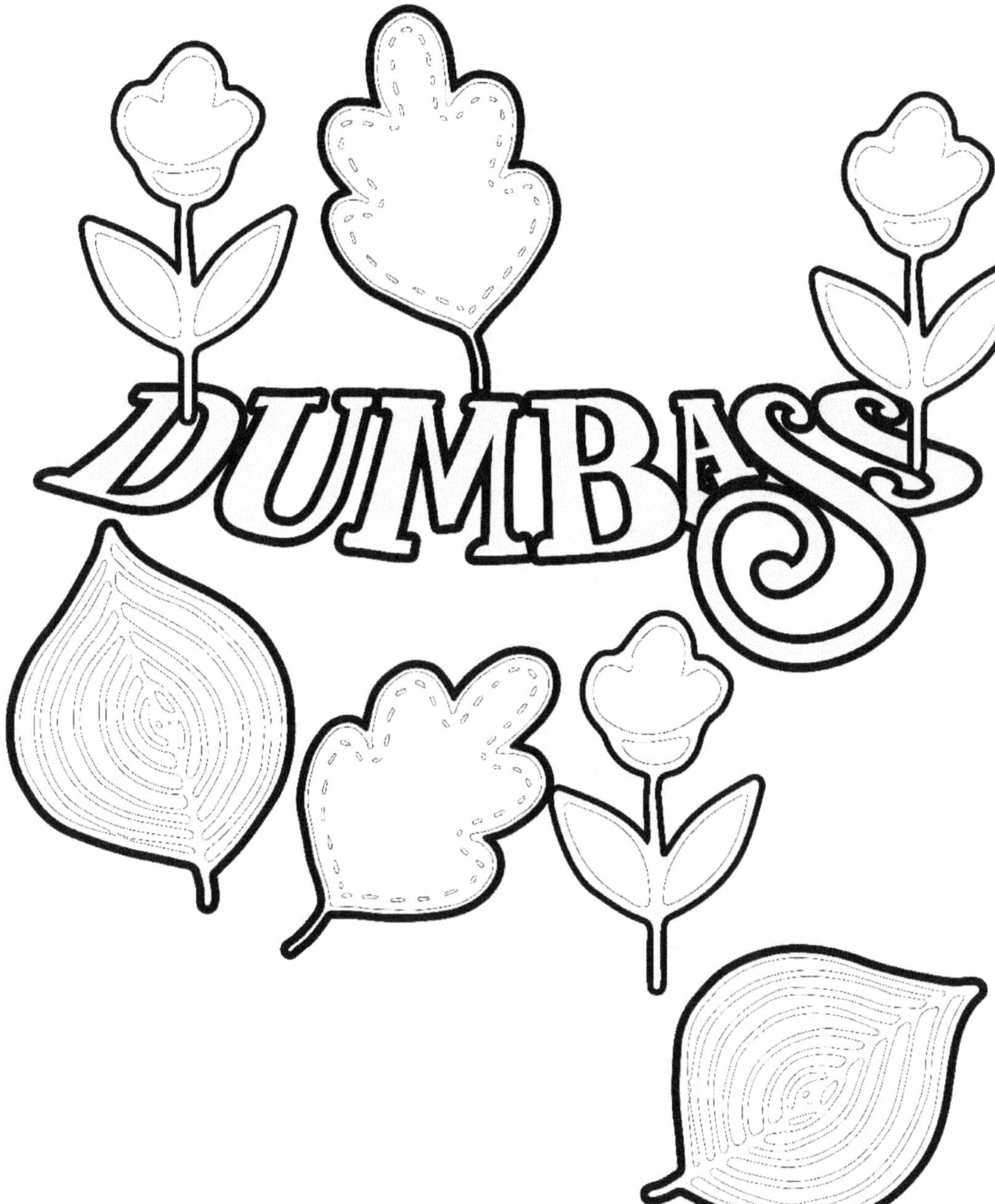
DUMBASS

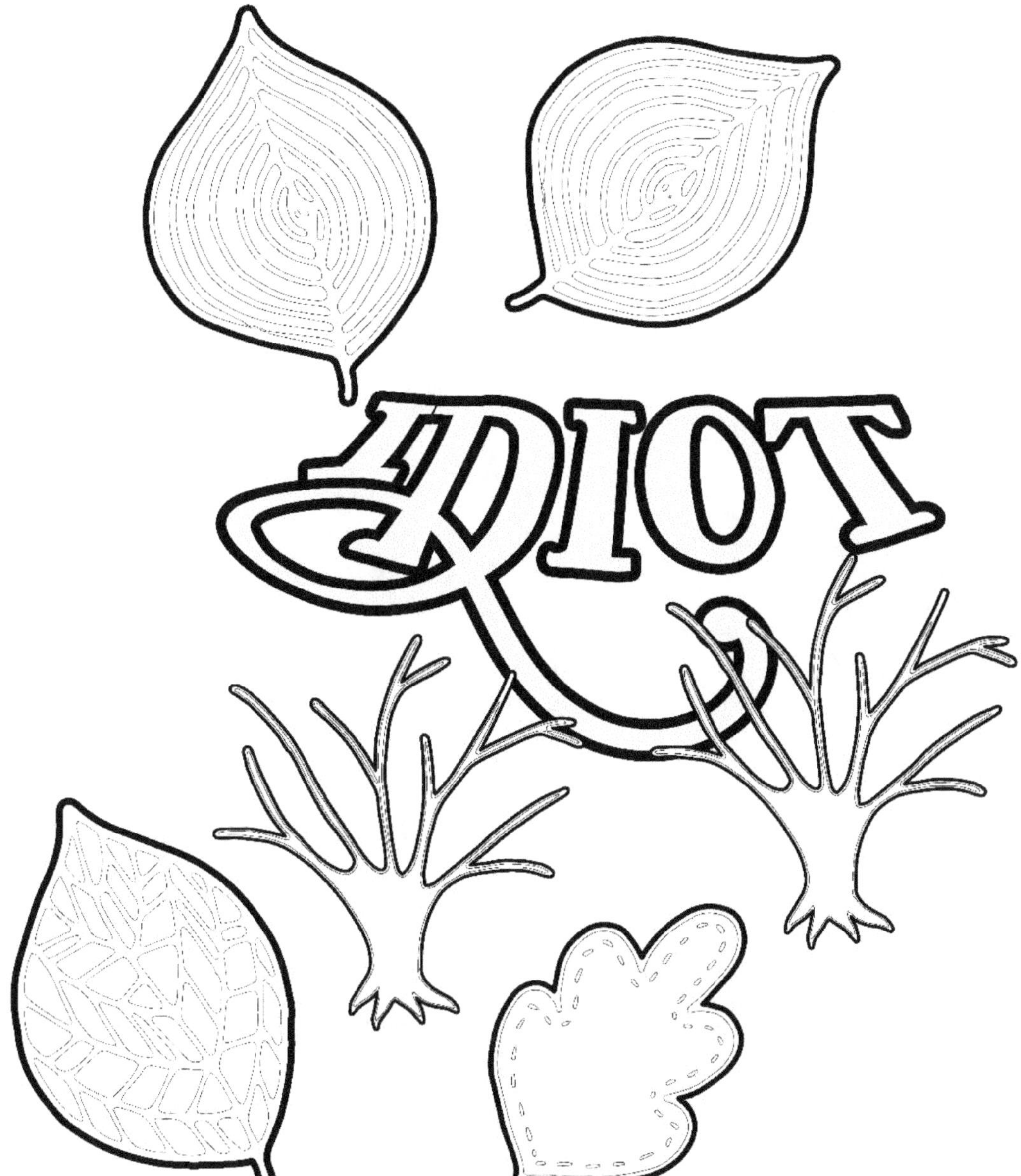
IDIOT

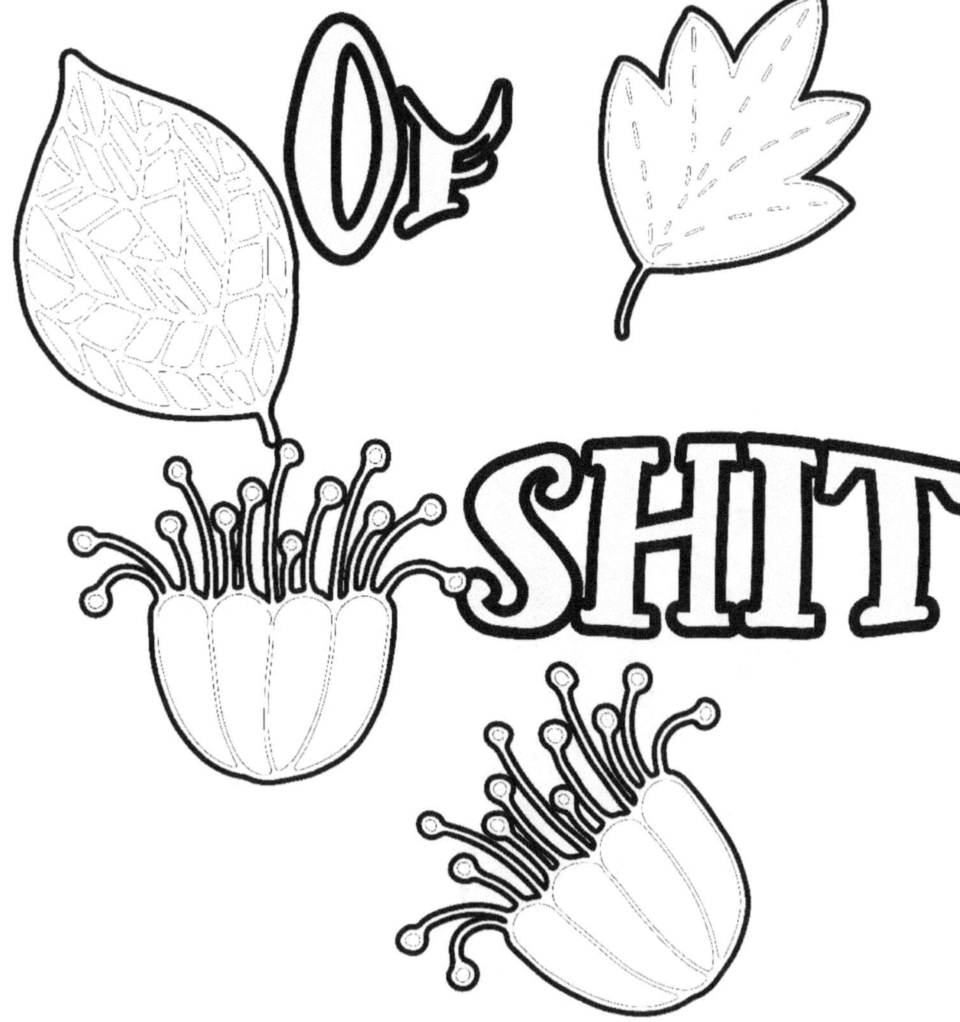
PIECE
OF
SHIT

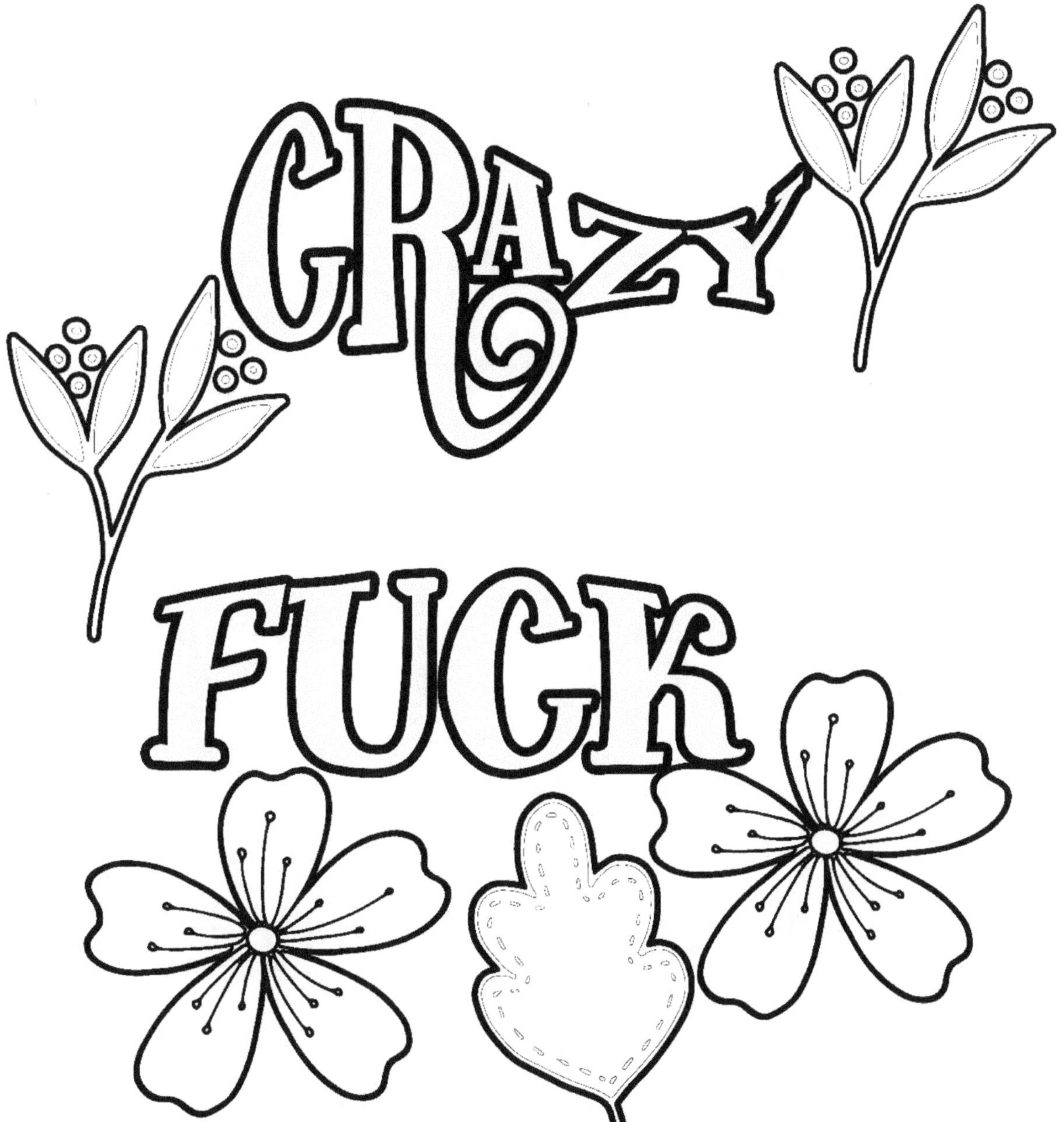
CRAZY
FUCK

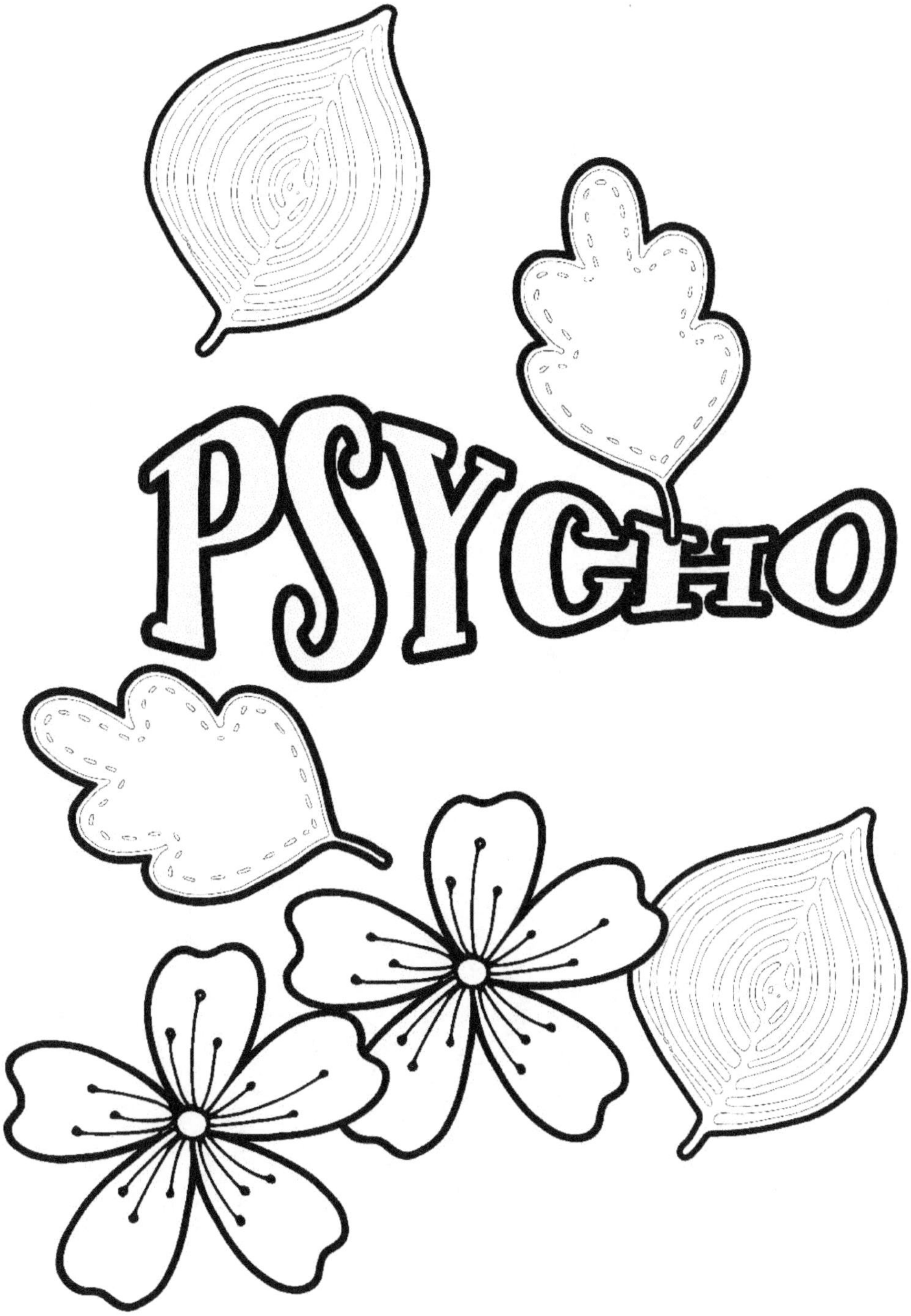
PSYCHO

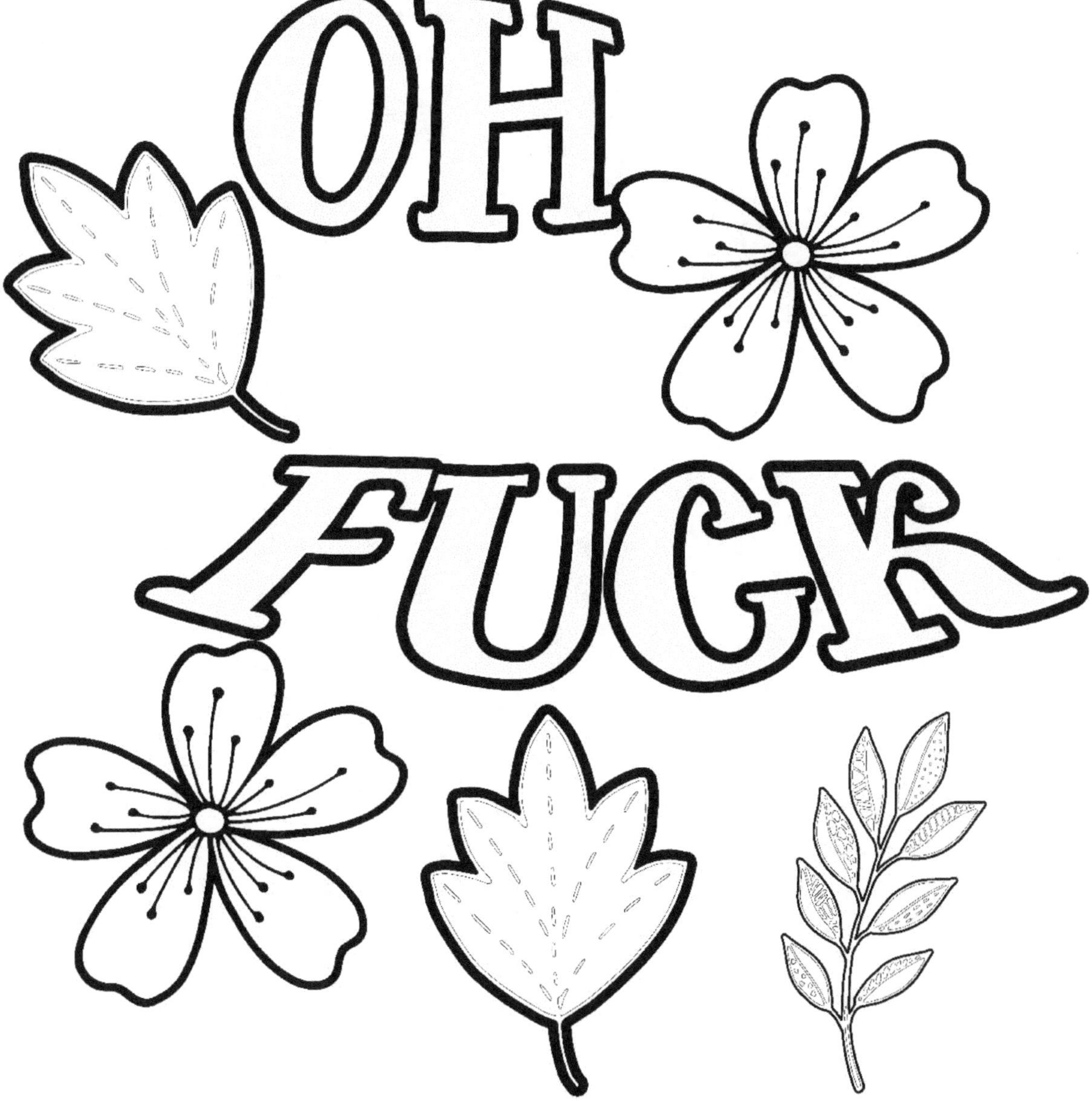
OH
FUCK

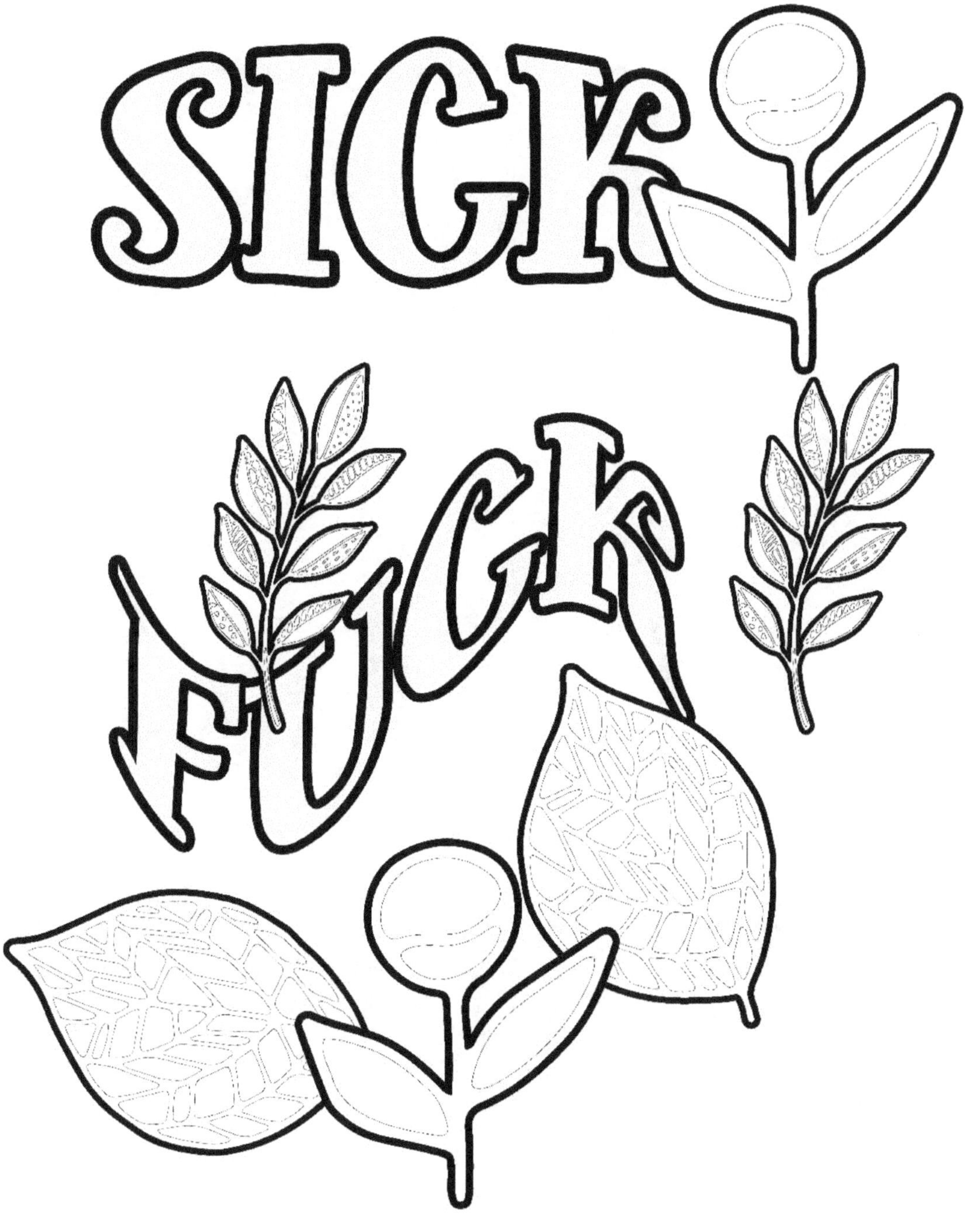
SICK
FUCK

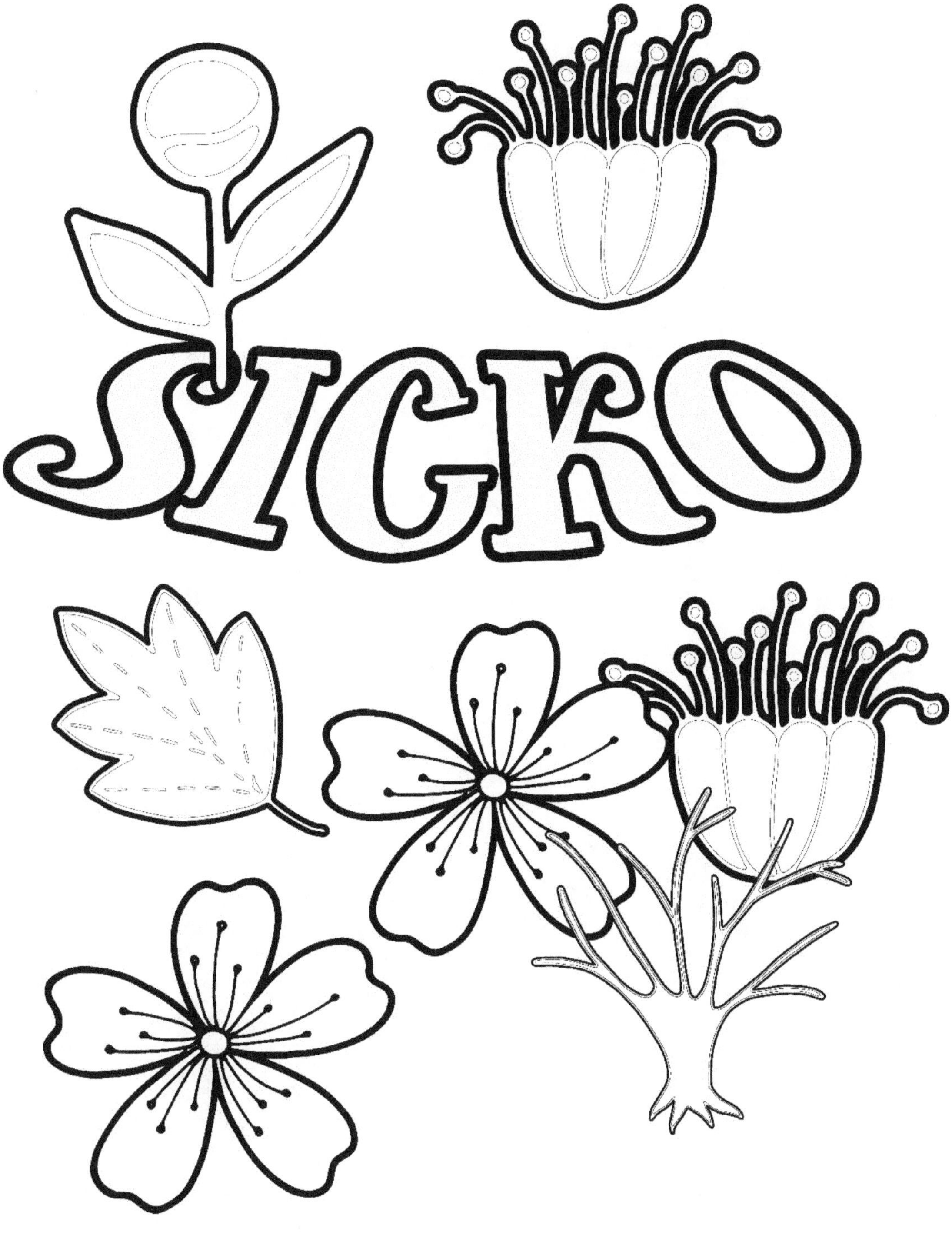
SICKO

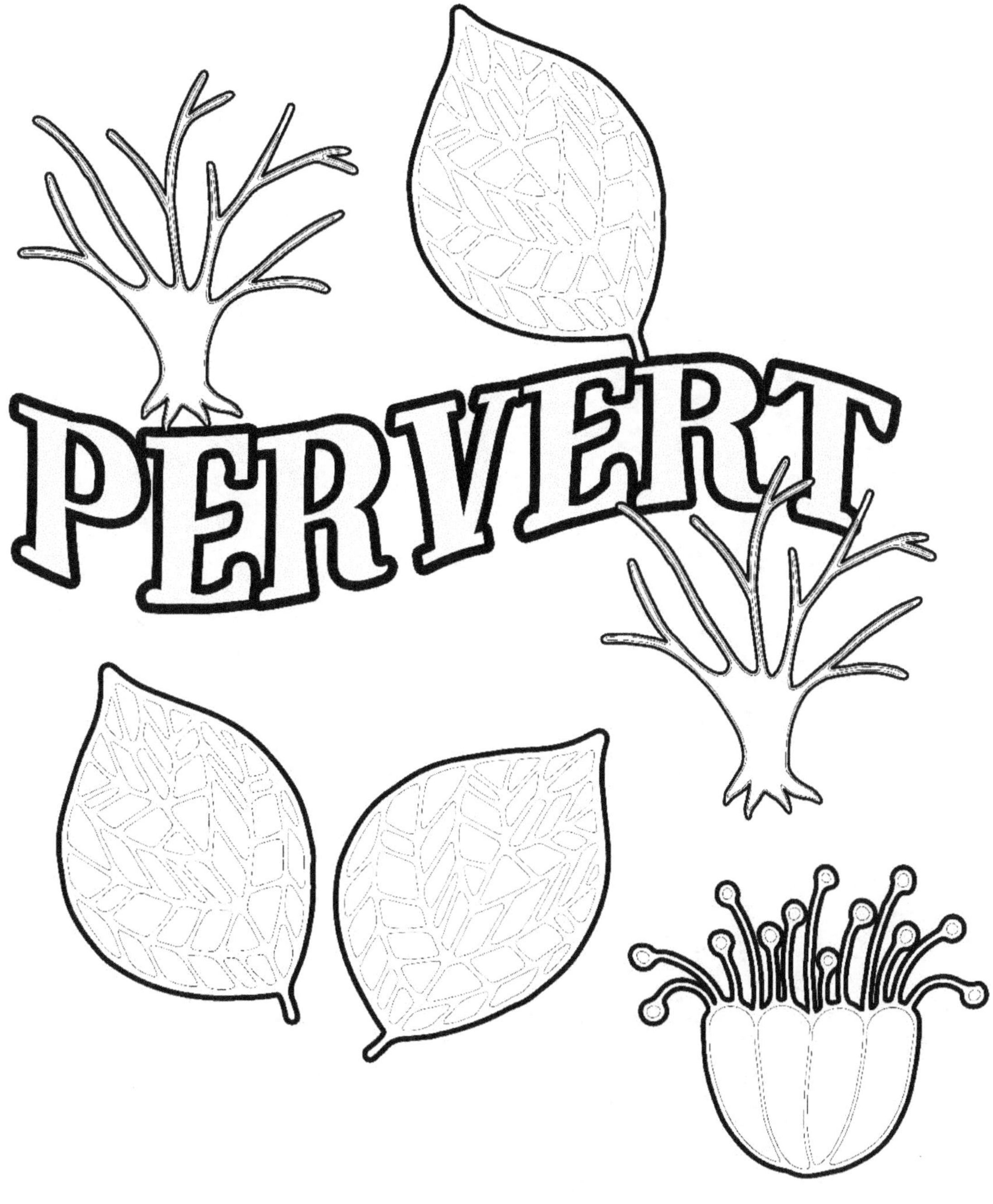
PERVERT

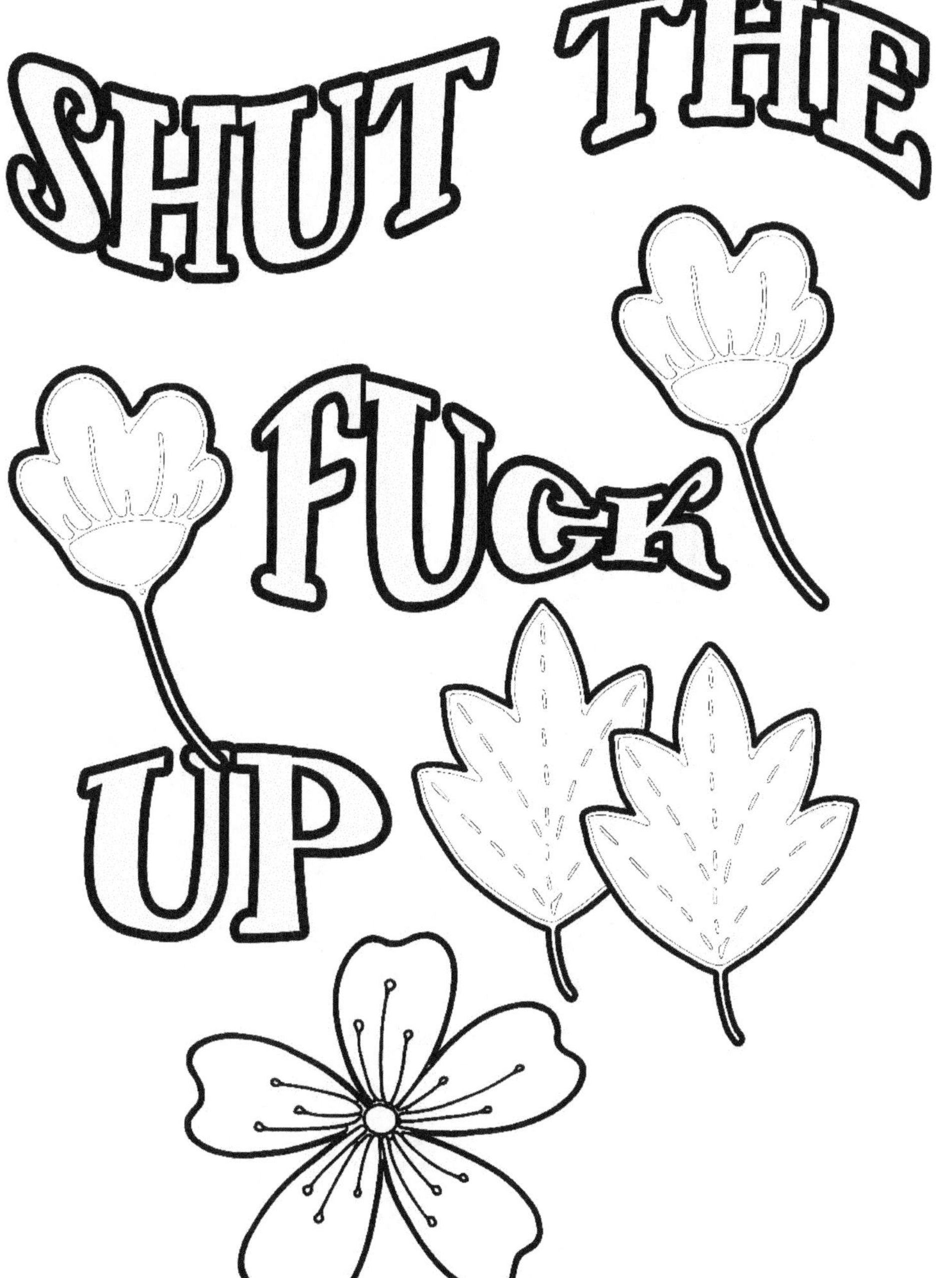
SHUT THE
fUck
UP

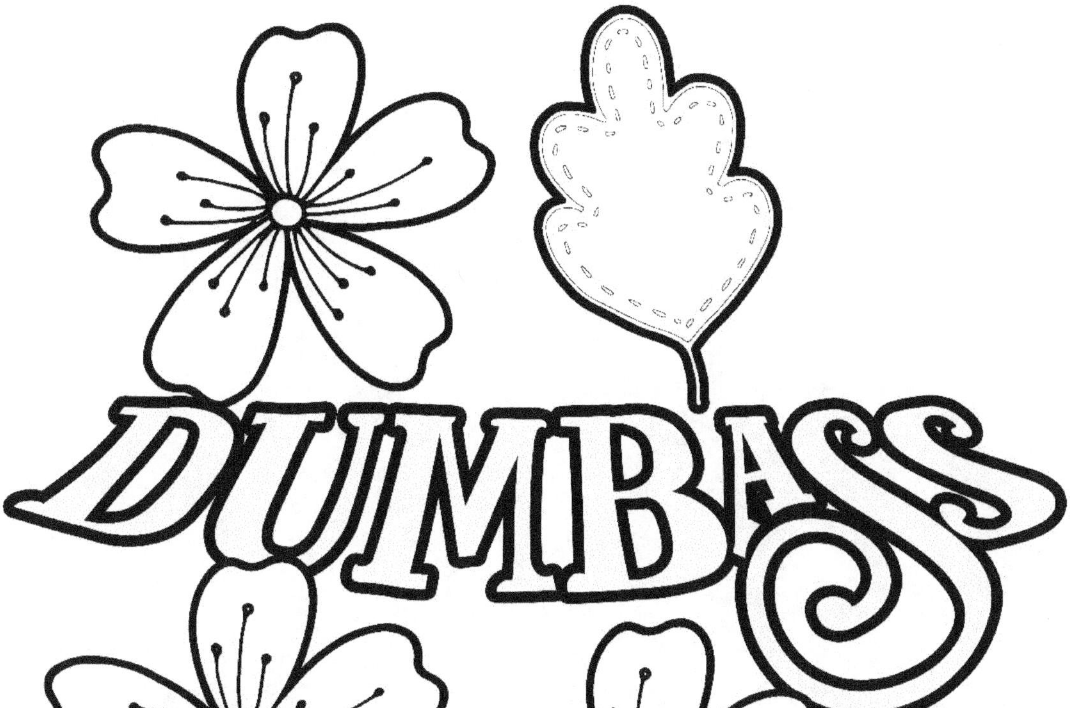
DUMBASS

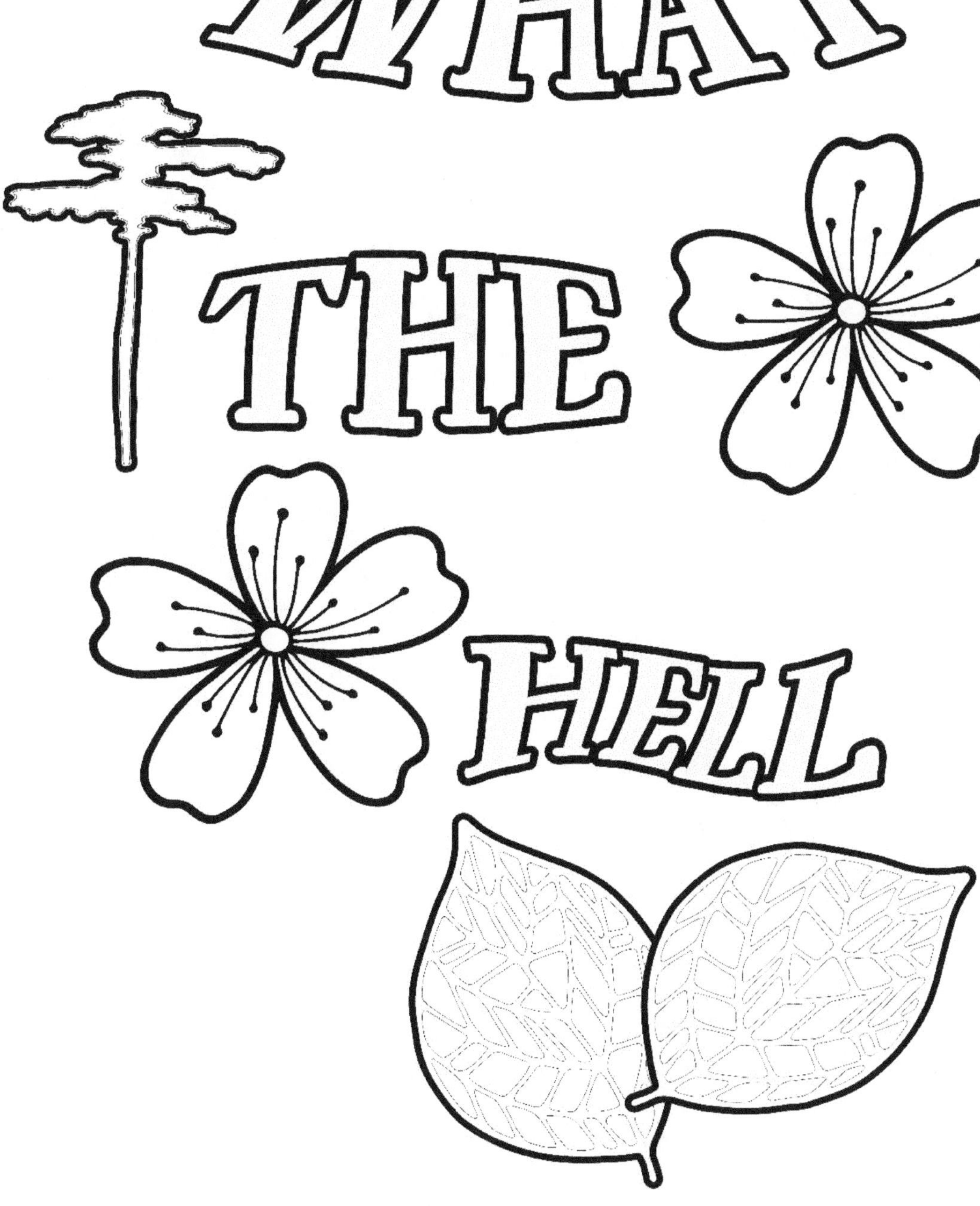
WHAT
THE
HELL

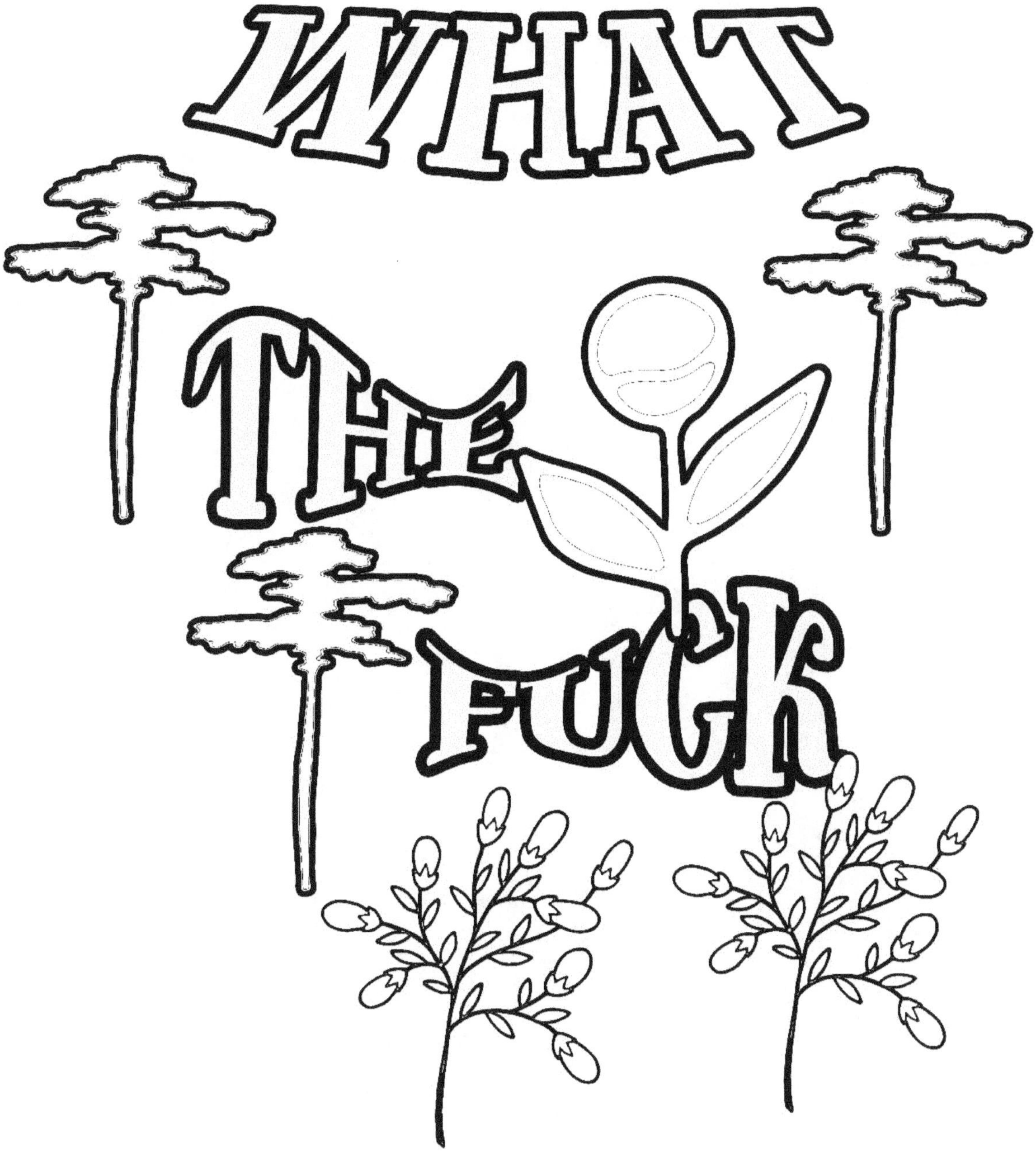
WHAT
THE
FUCK

Note

www.ingramcontent.com/pod-product-compliance
Lightning Source LLC
Chambersburg PA
CBHW080642190526
45169CB00009B/3472